A World
of Love for
Animals

Dedicated to all living, feeling beings
and their freedom from pain.

—Ingrid Newkirk

Table of Contents

Foreword

Even before I appeared in that little movie you may have heard of about a talking pig, I believed that all animals—from pigs to primates to parakeets—deserve our compassion and respect. I felt in my heart that their lives are important and not mine to take, which led me to go vegetarian (and, later, vegan) decades ago. I sensed kindred spirits in the folks at PETA, who have made a name for themselves pushing the envelope for animal protection—a strategy some might think is risky. But it's hard to argue with success: PETA is now the leading animal rights organization in the world and works hard to keep growing.

From its modest, no-frills headquarters in Norfolk, Virginia, which I have had the pleasure of visiting (Spoiler alert: There are dogs *everywhere*), PETA orchestrates an international network of affiliates, activists, supporters, and volunteers who achieve awe-inspiring victories for animals all over the globe.

I am proud to have played a role in some of those victories. Back in 2001, I participated in a PETA sit-in at a Wendy's restaurant to protest the fast-food chain's hideously wanting animal-care standards, including the almost unimaginable barbarism of confining mother pigs to stalls so small that they couldn't even turn around, much less take more than a single step in any direction.

No one needs to have a conversation with Babe to know that pigs suffer if they are kept virtually immobilized for months on end. Like us, they long to stretch their legs, get out into the fresh air, and socialize with their friends and family. That doesn't seem like too much to ask, does it? We didn't think so, and we said it and said it again, until finally police officers arrived to lead us away in handcuffs—but not before we had gotten our point across. Shortly afterward, Wendy's announced plans to purchase pig flesh only from farms that don't confine smart, sensitive, sociable pigs to absurdly minuscule crates. It's a start.

That wasn't the only time I was arrested for defending animals' rights. Along with a PETA staffer, I was arrested for interrupting a Board of Regents meeting at the University of Wisconsin–Madison. We went there to protest the school's cruel brain experiments on cats. PETA had obtained dozens of heartbreaking photographs showing the miserable life and death of one of them, a beautiful ginger tabby named Double Trouble. She was tortured for months, subjected to invasive surgeries on her ears, skull, and brain.

Laboratory records revealed that Double Trouble's anesthetics wore off during one surgery. She woke up to what must have been an excruciatingly painful and terrifying ordeal as experimenters cut into her skull. After PETA told the world what she and the other cats at UW-Madison had endured, the ensuing public outrage prompted this awful laboratory to close its doors.

When I turned 75, I could think of no better way to celebrate than to advocate for animals, which is what I did, by speaking at PETA's Capitol Hill congressional briefing on the National Institutes of Health's (NIH) maternal-deprivation experiments on baby monkeys. In these kinds of sadistic experiments, newborn monkeys are torn away from their loving mothers, terrorized with loud sounds and realistic-looking fake snakes, addicted to alcohol, and forced to live alone in small cages in order to worsen their psychological distress. Months later, I got the best belated birthday present ever when NIH announced that it was pulling the plug on that set of horrific experiments.

I remember back to PETA's very first campaign—the precedent-setting 1981 Silver Spring monkeys case—which resulted in the first arrest and criminal conviction of an animal experimenter in the U.S. on charges of cruelty to animals, the first confiscation of abused animals from a laboratory, and the first U.S. Supreme Court victory for animals used in experiments. PETA has never stopped fighting—and winning—in their efforts to save animals, and I'm with them all the way. That's why I would go to the ends of the Earth for them—because I know that they'll go just as far to defend animals. But you don't have to take my word for it. You can see for yourself what PETA has accomplished for animals all over the world. A good place to start is with the inspiring rescue stories in this book.

—James Cromwell

Introduction

Years ago, when I was serving as Washington, D.C.'s "poundmaster," a call came in about a neglect case. I rushed to the address that the caller had given and was greeted by a pitiful sight: A little dog, tail tucked between her legs, had been left chained outside to shiver and quake all night long in the bitter, freezing cold. She had no doghouse to huddle inside, no straw to provide any insulation from the biting wind. All she had was a blanket—which was worse than nothing at all, because it had frozen solid. She probably would have frozen out there, too, if I hadn't scooped her up and rushed her back to the shelter.

Once the little dog had warmed up and eaten a good meal and was dozing peacefully, I lamented to one of my fellow shelter workers, "How could anyone possibly be so mean?" She shook her head. Like most people who work in the animal protection field, she had seen some of the ugliest abuse that our species is capable of doling out. But then she said something I'll never forget: "The thing to remember is that for every cruelty case we are alerted to, there was a kind person out there who cared enough to call us."

It was one of those "lightbulb moments." In the more than four decades since then, my work for animal rights has taken me all over the world— from the slums of Mumbai to slaughterhouses in Taiwan to a homeless encampment along the Los

Angeles freeway. Wherever I go, a few things remain remarkably consistent: There are always animals in need, and while some people are indeed cruel, there are always many who are kind and want to help.

I've stopped my car on the shoulder of a busy highway after seeing a lost dog running dangerously close to the traffic whizzing past—only to have one, two, or even three other motorists pull over and work in tandem with me to rescue the terrified pup. They didn't hesitate—they saw an emergency unfolding and jumped right in.

On another occasion, I found a fawn lying by the side of the road, after someone had hit her and kept on driving. Her leg was shattered, and she was thrashing desperately, in severe pain and scared out of her wits. For nearly an hour, I stayed by her side, running into the street, waving my arms, and yelling whenever a vehicle approached, to try to flag down some help. But not one person stopped. You just never know who has a heart and who doesn't.

I know that PETA's staff all over the world have hearts. I've seen them tear up the very shirt they were wearing to make a bandage for a dog with a slashed paw and risk their own lives to jump into a truck full of exhausted bullocks, turn them around, and guide them out to safety. I've seen them wade through contaminated floodwaters in the aftermath of a hurricane to reach petrified kittens who were mewing at the top of their lungs and clinging for dear life to a patio umbrella. I've even seen them transform from Clark Kent into Superman … or at least I've seen a mild-mannered staff member in Taiwan scale a 30-foot-high fence, seemingly in a single bound, to reach animals who needed help.

It's all because they care so deeply—and because they know that a kind person's intervention can mean the difference between life and a painful death for animals in danger. This book is full of stories like these.

You don't need a red cape, superhuman abilities, or even any special talent to make a world of difference for animals in need. All you need is compassion and the willingness to help. It can be as simple as picking up the phone to report cruelty, giving a thirsty dog a drink, or helping a turtle get safely across the road. The stakes for animals are far too high for us to stay silent, look the other way, keep on driving, or assume that "someone else will help." Animals need every one of us to be that person who cares—and helps!

I thank everyone who takes action to help animals. And I know that, if they could, the animals would thank you, too.

Ingrid Newkirk
President
People for the Ethical Treatment of Animals

Chapter 1

A Taal Tale

No one at PETA Asia will ever forget January 12, 2020. It was on that day that they watched in horror from their headquarters in the Philippines as Taal volcano erupted for the first time in more than 40 years, spewing smoke and lava 9 miles into the air.

The staff was well acquainted with the community surrounding the volcano, located on a tiny island in the middle of Taal Lake. For years, PETA Asia and International Veterinary Outreach had teamed up to operate free medical clinics for the horses who were forced to haul tourists up and down the volcano's steep slopes as well as for the cats, dogs, and other animals who lived on the island. One "community dog" named Palakitik had always had a special place in the hearts of the PETA Asia team, trotting out to greet them as soon as they arrived and following them as they made their rounds.

The humans on the island were evacuated when the eruptions began, but the animals were left to fend for themselves. PETA Asia staffers were beside themselves with worry about Palakitik and all the other animals who had been left behind to face the volcano's wrath.

PETA Asia pleaded with government and military officials to let them take their skiff across the lake to rescue the animal survivors, but they were turned away as the threat of another eruption loomed. They were told that the animals were probably dead, but they vowed to keep trying.

As PETA Asia Senior Vice President Jason Baker put it, "We're PETA, so 'no' means 'try harder.'" Within 48 hours, they had arrived on the island. Their hearts sank as they surveyed the devastated beach. The emerald green palm trees and thatch-roofed huts were gone, replaced by a gray hellscape engulfed in acrid smoke and mounds of smoldering ash.

Hundreds of animals died in the eruption, including many of the horses the team had helped for so long. The bodies of the dead were scattered everywhere, and the air reeked of their decomposing flesh. Surviving animals cowered under collapsed structures or wandered about in shock and confusion.

"Palakitik?" PETA Asia's Jana Sevilla called out, trying to keep her voice steady. Silence. "Palakitik?" she called again. Were her eyes playing tricks on her? She watched in disbelief as a small brown figure hurtled down the beach toward her. Palakitik's eyes were almost stuck shut with gray ash, but she raced toward Jana's voice. "PALAKITIK!" This time it wasn't a question. She fell to her knees and threw her arms around the floppy-eared dog, tears streaming down her face and melting into soft fur caked with ash. "I love you, silly, pretty girl."

PETA Asia staffers rescued almost 200 animals stranded on Taal island, filling their small boat with puppies, cats, goats, pigs, horses, and even wildlife—crisscrossing the lake until all were ferried to safety. The animals needed medical treatment for inflamed eyes, skin burned by falling ash, and lungs damaged by thick smoke. After they healed, they were placed with loving families.

But Palakitik was never put up for adoption. That's because she went home with Jana, who couldn't bear the thought of never seeing her friend again. Palakitik still enjoys regular visits with PETA Asia staffers. But now, the visits are purely social in nature.

Chapter 2

BUZZ GOES TO INFINITY AND BEYOND

When Buzz arrived at the PETA-supported veterinary clinic in Petra, Jordan, the dejected little donkey was in such tremendous pain that he could barely stand up. His body was covered with wounds, including a hideously large burn on his shoulder.

Petra is a UNESCO World Heritage site, but that means little to donkeys like Buzz who spend their days hauling tourists around the ruins of the ancient city under the scorching desert sun. It may be the 21st century, but for the 1,300 or more animals used in the tourist trade in Petra, it might as well be 300 B.C.

Little donkeys, most malnourished and some even lame, are forced to climb 900 crumbling stone steps up to Petra's monastery and then back down again with tourists on their backs. And some tourists weigh a lot. If the animals falter, they're whipped. Horses are forced to pull heavy carriages on a grueling, rocky, 6-mile trek five or more times a day—every single day—in the blazing sun

15

without any water or shade.

When PETA first traveled to Petra in 2017, we saw donkeys and horses being hit in the head with rocks, jabbed with pointed sticks that brought blood, and viciously lashed with chains or whips just for going too slow. We saw ropes encrusted with blood from digging into the animals' necks and metal halters cutting into their noses. Between rides, some animals were tied up so tightly that they couldn't lie down.

We took our findings to government authorities, and they said all the right things, pledging to improve conditions for animals and to stop wanton abuse. But when a PETA investigator returned to Petra a year later, the animals, like the city itself, appeared to be trapped in time: Nothing had changed. Nothing!

Something had to be done. Since officials were unwilling to budge on the idea of abandoning the archaic use of donkeys, camels, and horses as transport for tourists, PETA decided to open a veterinary clinic for these long-suffering animals, the only facility of its kind in this vast region of barren rocks. On call 24 hours a day, a team led by Dr. Hassan Shata, an excellent equine surgeon from Egypt, provides dozens of animals with free services every day, treating every condition imaginable, from lameness and hoof deformities to abscesses and severe wounds like burns and stabbings—some deliberately inflicted—as well as giving them the food, water, and rest that they desperately need.

Dr. Hassan took one look at Buzz's shoulder and came to a depressing conclusion: The little donkey must have been ruthlessly electroshocked with a stun gun repeatedly in a barbaric attempt to force him to keep working. In addition to the painful burns, his muscles were so severely damaged that he was unable to stand without assistance, and his breathing and heartbeat were both dangerously erratic. But that wasn't even the worst of it—he had been deprived of nutritious food for so long that he had resorted to eating plastic trash in a futile attempt to ease his hunger pangs, wreaking havoc on his digestive system, clogging his intestines, and causing an excruciatingly painful rectal prolapse.

Dr. Hassan and his staff immediately went to work trying to save Buzz's life, administering painkillers, antibiotics, IV fluids, and laxatives. They cleaned and bandaged his wounds and repaired his prolapsed rectum, allowing him to pass the chunks of plastic that would have killed him.

Buzz, who had known nothing but misery in his short life, had every reason to give up. But he kept on fighting, stoically submitting to a daily physical therapy regimen to help strengthen his ravaged muscles, including slow, careful walks led by patient clinic staffers. Over the weeks, Buzz steadily improved, until one day, he was finally able to stand on his own and eat some solid food. Just imagine what that first bite of fresh barley must have tasted like to him!

Keenly intelligent and prone to careful contemplation before acting, donkeys like Buzz have a reason behind every decision they make. These sociable animals often greet one another by gently blowing in each other's faces. Humans often disparage a donkey's caution as "stubbornness," but donkeys are inquisitive and ready to take on new experiences—on their own terms. Who could fault them for that?

Now a permanent resident and unofficial "greeter" at the clinic, Buzz has become best friends with one of the clinic's resident dogs, Sultan, whom he loves to "stealth groom" while Sultan is napping. Buzz is safe now, but other animals still suffer terribly in Petra. Unlike the tourists they carry on their backs, they never get a vacation. As long as people thoughtlessly book animal rides, donkeys, horses, and camels will still be forced to work until they literally drop from exhaustion—and PETA will do its best to be there to pick them up.

"[C]ompassion, in which ethics takes root, does not assume its true proportions until it embraces not only man but every living being."

—Albert Schweitzer

Chapter 3

A Camel Without a Hump

It's not every day that you see a camel in your neighborhood, even in parts of India. So when Samarth showed up in a small village in Maharashtra, villagers didn't know quite what to make of him. The wooden peg driven through his nostrils was evidence that he had been forced to work—yanked this way and that by a rope tied to the peg, probably either to make him "dance" in a circus or cart tourists around on his back. But he was in no condition to work—and hadn't been for quite some time. He was old and ill, which likely led to his being cast aside like an old shoe.

No one knows how long Samarth—weak, bewildered, and blind in one eye—had wandered in search of food. His face, neck, and legs were riddled with mange, and his body was covered with open sores, including one on the sole of his foot that made taking each step a painful struggle. He was so starved and dehydrated that his skin was stretched taut—making every rib and vertebra stand out—and his hump (made up of stored fat) had almost completely disappeared.

When a group of schoolchildren spotted Samarth, they began taunting the defenseless animal, pelting him with stones and hitting him with sticks. Desperate to escape the abuse, he managed to muster what little strength he had left to flee, but he wasn't going to be able to get very far. Alerted by the ruckus, kind villagers rushed to his aid and chased the children off just as he was about to collapse from exhaustion. But now what? After some discussion, the group decided to call the forest department, the police, and a news reporter for help. As it turned out, alerting the media proved to be a fortuitous choice.

The reporter was familiar with the work of Animal Rahat, a PETA-supported rescue group that has made a name for itself providing working bullocks, donkeys, and other animals in India with lifesaving medical care and other aid. At the reporter's urging, the villagers phoned Animal Rahat's 24-hour emergency hotline, and soon help was on the way!

The team arrived with a spacious flatbed truck lined with soft sod and cushions fashioned out of grain sacks to protect his frail body during the bumpy journey to Animal Rahat's sanctuary. A veterinary team greeted Samarth upon his arrival, stroking his nose and whispering to him reassuringly as they got to work.

Today, Samarth is almost unrecognizable.

Although he will never regain the vision in his right eye and still bears the scar of the peg that once pierced his nose, he has regained the weight that he had lost (including his hump!) and has soft brown fur where there were once scabs and sores. He has made friends with the other camels who share his sanctuary home as well as the donkeys, cows, sheep, and dogs. He enjoys resting in the warm sunshine, rolling in the grass like an enormous dog, being groomed by his caretakers, and munching on his favorite snack: lush green leaves.

After rescuing Samarth and putting him on the road to recovery, the Animal Rahat team had one more vital task ahead. Knowing the importance of teaching children empathy and compassion, they returned to the village where he had been abandoned and presented a humane education workshop at the local school. They encouraged the children to imagine what it must have been like for Samarth to be lost, scared, and alone in a strange place and urged them to live by the Golden Rule—to treat others the way they would want to be treated.

The children who had harassed Samarth realized that they had been thoughtless and unkind and solemnly pledged never to harm another animal. School staff and parents were so impressed with the presentation that they invited Animal Rahat to return for an entire humane education series. The first lesson? Whenever anyone—human or camel—is down in the dumps, we should always help them get over the hump.

Chapter 4

'HURRICANE PEDRO' MAKES LANDFALL IN A NEW HOME

The injured puppy could only whimper and cower, absolutely terrified, as the 155-mph winds and driving rain of Hurricane Maria pummeled the crumbling animal shelter that had been his home ever since he was rescued from the streets of Guayama, Puerto Rico.

The hurricane had left an unprecedented trail of devastation in its wake. Buildings were swamped, roofs were torn off, and trees were tossed around like matchsticks, blocking roads and knocking out power and water supplies to most of the island. When disasters like this strike, PETA's Emergency Response Team is standing by to help the animals who are often at the bottom of first responders' to-do lists, mobilizing to help dogs, cats, farmed animals, wildlife, and others in the hardest-hit areas. Immediately after Hurricane Maria, there were no commercial flights and no boats willing to take passengers onto the island. So PETA pulled out all the stops, chartering a plane, thanks to a member's generosity, and flying to Puerto Rico as soon as authorities allowed the team entry.

The battered animal shelter where Pedro lived was one of their first stops. Team members brought food and other supplies; helped clear trees, repair damaged structures, and clean up the mess left behind by the wind and floodwaters; and, most importantly, gave the traumatized animals the assurance of safety and the help that they desperately needed. When a team member spotted Pedro, she knew right away that he was in bad shape: His front leg was swollen to more than twice its normal size. She carefully approached him, knowing that he was frightened and in a great deal of pain. But the brown-and-white puppy with the big floppy ears immediately began wagging his tail. When she gently picked him up, careful to avoid jostling his injured leg, he snuggled into her arms.

PETA's team spent two weeks rescuing animals in devastated areas, helping well over 1,000 of them. Before the team flew back to PETA's headquarters in Norfolk, Virginia, they loaded up some of the most vulnerable animals to take with them. That's how Pedro—in desperate need of emergency veterinary care and having won the hearts of team members with his undiminished good spirits—embarked on his very first plane trip. It was time for him and the other refugees to learn that there was more to life than cage bars and concrete floors.

Even after arriving in Virginia, Pedro still had a long journey of recovery ahead of him. The injury to his leg had gone untreated for weeks, perhaps months, and a serious infection had set in. Even with top-notch care, the infection lingered. His caretakers worried that his leg would have to be amputated. But Pedro wasn't about to give up. After months of treatment and many, many vet visits, his infection cleared up and he bounced back—and he hasn't stopped bouncing since.

Energetic and playful, Pedro has gone from a hurricane victim to a hurricane of activity. Adopted by a PETA staffer in Texas, when he first met his new "mom," he ran up to her and joyfully leaped right into her lap, as if she were a long-lost friend. He has now grown into his oversize ears and enjoys fetching a tennis ball, going on walks with his guardians, chewing on his many toys, and meeting up for playdates at the dog park. Pedro still loves snuggling and can often be found stretched out on a bed or a lap, enjoying some much-deserved TLC.

Chapter 5

SPECIAL DELIVERY: HELP JUST IN THE NICK OF TIME FOR JAYA AND HER BABY

It's almost too horrible to contemplate, but it really happened. When an Animal Rahat staffer spotted a pretty pony wandering forlornly down a street in Sangli, India, he noticed something so shocking he wouldn't have believed it if he hadn't seen it with his own eyes. Some cruel person or people had used thick copper wire to staple the pony's vulva closed. With every step Jaya took, pain shot through her body.

The perpetrators of this depraved act had likely used a "twitch," a vile device to stop horses and ponies from struggling to escape by tightly pinching their nostrils or lips. Jaya's extremely painful mutilation—an inept attempt to prevent her from being bred by a passing stallion—was not only appallingly cruel but also poorly timed. Unbeknownst to her tormenters, Jaya was already pregnant. In fact, she was just days away from giving birth! Can you imagine what would have happened if Animal Rahat had not found her?

The group filed a cruelty-to-animals report with the local police, and while officers and the local news media looked on, the team set to work alleviating the little pony's suffering. Based on her past experiences, Jaya had every reason to distrust humans, and no one would have blamed her for lashing out with a well-placed kick. Instead, showing great poise and self-control, she calmly stood stock-still as an Animal Rahat veterinarian administered a sedative, then ever so delicately snipped the wires. The only signs of her distress were an occasional flinch and stomp of her foot. After the last staple was removed and the wounds cleaned, she swished her long tail as Animal Rahat staffers gently stroked her neck and congratulated her on being so brave.

The team consulted with a government veterinarian, who provided police with a statement supporting their assessment that what had been done to Jaya was an act of egregious cruelty that must be prosecuted and punished. The police were never able to track down her abusers, but the search has never stopped. Those responsible had likely been forcing her to participate in cruel pony cart races, in which "joyriders" beat and bully animals to make them run until they drop from exhaustion. One common practice is hitching a pony to the same cart as a bullock, something that's extremely dangerous (not to mention illegal).

Animal Rahat took legal custody of Jaya and pledged to protect her for the rest of her life.

Just days after moving into her new home at the group's peaceful 10-acre sanctuary, Jaya gave birth to a handsome colt—a happy, healthy baby named Rudi who is now growing up at his mother's side, blissfully unaware that his life was nearly over before it even began. Without Animal Rahat's timely intervention, it's unlikely that either Jaya or Rudi would be alive today.

Mother and son are thriving at the sanctuary, where they have plenty of room to run and graze. And just as important to these highly social animals, they can interact with each other and the other sanctuary residents, including Marguerite, another pony who, believe it or not, endured the same atrocious mutilation as Jaya and also survived, thanks to Animal Rahat.

Chapter 6

THIS ARROW GOES STRAIGHT TO THE HEART

S haking ground. Shattered glass. A thunderous boom. Any of us would instinctively run and hide from a terrifying blast—unless we were restrained by a chain.

On August 4, 2020, Beirut's busy port was rocked by a massive explosion: 2,700 tons of ammonium nitrate detonated in one of the largest non-nuclear blasts in history. The explosion was so loud it could be heard all the way across the Mediterranean Sea. Much of the city was blanketed in dust and rubble. Roads were littered with glass shards and bricks. Hospitals were inundated with injured and dying people—it's estimated that 6,500 people were injured and 200 died.

Of course, those figures reflect only the human lives affected. Scores of dogs, cats, chickens, and other animals were hurt or sent fleeing in terror. Just hours after news of the disaster reverberated around the world, PETA U.K. went into emergency response mode, supporting local animal-care organizations in reuniting lost animals with their families and sending campaign team member Theodora Iona to Beirut to help with rescue efforts. Theodora was warned to stay away because of civil unrest, but she didn't, instead delivering critically needed dog and cat food to families whose homes had been damaged or destroyed and to local first responders working to ensure that displaced or abandoned animals wouldn't go hungry. Her first rescue was of an injured chicken she named Doris and delivered to a veterinarian for care.

As she combed through the streets, Theodora called out to shell-shocked animals. Some were hiding, and many were dehydrated from the summer heat. Then there was Arrow, an elderly dog with white whiskers and sad brown eyes who sat dejected at the end of a chain, trying to stay out of the burning sun by burrowing under a rusty metal shed, his only "shelter." Arrow would have heard and felt the explosion but not been able to run or hide from it. He would have watched humans escape the destruction but wouldn't have been able to flee alongside them.

He had spent much of his life being treated like an unpaid security guard, faithfully barking to alert his owner to potential threats but receiving precious little in return. He was kept chained up in the blistering sun all day long, all summer long. He had clearly been deprived of food and was so malnourished that Theodora could see the outline of his ribs showing through his fur.

Locals told her that the man who owned him was connected to Hezbollah, and she was warned against trying to contact him. But she was determined not to leave Arrow there in that condition. This poor old dog deserved a chance at a comfortable life, and she vowed to make it happen.

Somehow, knowing so much rode on her success, Theodora managed to charm the fierce man into giving her the dog! She rushed Arrow to a veterinary clinic, where he was treated while she lined up a new home for him. It didn't take long, thanks to a local animal rights volunteer who knew just the right family for him! Arrow had no idea where he was going, but he seemed to understand that something great was finally going to happen to him. Theodora still remembers the look of joy and excitement on his face as he leapt into her car. He relished the journey, looking eagerly out the window, inhaling fresh air, and enjoying what may have been the first adventure of his life.

Life with his new family in the hills outside Beirut bears no resemblance to his former life on a chain. Arrow runs and plays in a spacious yard with his new canine friends—three boisterous young dogs who make him feel like a puppy again. His tail wags virtually nonstop, just like a metronome.

His former life of privation is starting to feel like ancient history. After all, time flies like an arrow once you've found the happiness you've been waiting for.

Chapter 7

Badal's Bad Old Days Are Behind Him

Something was very wrong. Everything hurt. Yet no matter how hard Badal tried to get the message across that he needed help, his handler kept pushing him harder.

Day after interminable day, the old horse hauled tourists through the hot, congested streets of Mumbai, dodging speeding cars and motorbikes and breathing in toxic exhaust fumes. The horse-drawn carriage (an ornate, silver-plated vehicle called a Victoria) was heavy, and the tackle dug into his skin. He was always hungry and thirsty, but his driver rarely stopped long enough to let him eat or drink.

Horses are herd animals who are keenly aware of their surroundings, and Badal had seen other horses collapse from exhaustion and be repeatedly whipped in an effort to get them back on their feet. He must have known that he was in for that kind of abuse if he faltered. For Victoria operators, making money mattered above all. Horses were viewed as little more than four-legged taxicabs to be worked until they broke down and couldn't haul one more passenger.

As the years went by, Badal grew weaker. His joints hurt with every step, his eyes burned from the dust and car exhaust, and his feet felt as if they were being jabbed with hot pokers. Yet the driver still forced him to work all day and well into the night.

By the time PETA India's Emergency Response Team heard about Badal's plight and intervened, every waking moment caused him misery. Not only was he coping with severe osteoarthritis, he also was suffering from a degenerative joint disorder called "ringbone," which develops when excess bone growth accumulates in leg joints. As if that painful condition weren't bad enough, all four of Badal's feet had "thrush," an infection so advanced that the tissue in his hooves had turned black and almost completely rotted away.

Cases like Badal's are why PETA India began a campaign to end this cruel trade through protests, advertising, multiple investigations, and legal actions. PETA President Ingrid Newkirk once hitched herself to a Victoria and "pulled" it through the streets of Mumbai to demonstrate how terribly horses struggled.

PETA India investigations documented injured, sick, and severely malnourished horses in the Victoria industry. When not pulling carriages, horses were housed in filthy, damp stables. They stood in their own waste, never had a moment's relief from biting insects, and never saw a veterinarian.

PETA India provided the Bombay High Court with the evidence that it had gathered, including expert veterinary testimony that forcing horses to toil long hours on asphalt was making them lame. The court agreed, ruling that using Victorias in Mumbai for "joyrides" was illegal. The days of the Victoria were over!

PETA India officials worked with authorities to get Badal confiscated from his abuser, then took him to a sanctuary operated by Animal Rahat. There, his caretakers were shocked by how debilitated he was. For the first few days, they braced for the worst, unsure if he would even survive. He had been worked nearly to death.

Today, Badal is living the good life at the sanctuary. His days have gone from constant toil to all the rest and relaxation a tired old horse could yearn for. Never again will he haul a carriage, feel the sting of the whip, stand on burning-hot pavement, dodge traffic, or be denied the simple pleasures of resting in the shade and socializing with his equine friends.

Chapter 8

THE PUP AND THE PAPER CUP

As a child, many of us had a "security blanket," a familiar item that brought us comfort. For puppies, it might be a stuffed toy, a blanket, or a littermate. But for Mogli, it was a crumpled paper cup.

This tiny puppy—struggling to survive by himself on the streets of Romania—must have pined for security and warmth, but he had no siblings to snuggle with and no mother to care for him. One dirty cup—perhaps flung from a car window or blown out of a trash can—was his only source of comfort in a big, scary world, and he carried it with him everywhere.

Little Mogli was all alone, but some 600,000 dogs and countless cats endure an equally harrowing existence on Romania's streets. Often plagued by mange and hunger, many succumb to a slow death from starvation, disease, or injuries.

But there is hope. PETA Germany's "PETA Helps Romania" program is tackling this crisis head-on by spaying, neutering, and licensing thousands of animals in Romania every year and providing veterinary treatment, food, and other

41

care.

With so many animals in need and a bounty on stray dogs' heads, compassionate people pick up animals off the streets and take them to "shelters." But conditions at these severely crowded, overburdened, and underfunded facilities are often *worse* than they are on the streets: Animals are crammed together in filthy, rusty cages without enough food or water. In winter, they shiver in frigid temperatures.

And since animals aren't separated or sterilized, they often mate and give birth right there in the shelters—adding to Romania's severe animal overpopulation problem. On the other hand, many animals who enter the shelters are so badly neglected that they don't even survive the ordeal.

But Mogli escaped that fate. One day, rescuers with PETA Germany's Romanian partner organization, Eduxanima, spotted what they nearly mistook for a piece of shag rug on a busy street. It was Mogli! He was so filthy and matted that he didn't even look like a living being. It's a miracle that no one had run him over.

One of the rescuers, Razvan, crouched down and slowly crept toward him, trying to appear as nonthreatening as possible. Mogli whimpered, unable to contain the mixture of excitement and fear swirling inside him. Would this man help him? Or would he yell and throw stones, as others had?

Although he was only a few months old,

Mogli's experience on the streets told him that he'd better not wait around to find out. He tried to flee, but he didn't get very far: The little puppy had rickets, a disease caused by a vitamin deficiency. He couldn't run or even walk—he was so weak he could barely crawl.

Razvan gently scooped him up, and Mogli's fears began to melt away. Realizing that he was safe at last, the little pup relaxed into the man's arms. Cami, another rescuer, searched the area in case Mogli's mother was hiding nearby, but she was nowhere to be found. Judging by his pitiful condition, it looked like he had been on his own for some time.

They took Mogli to PETA Germany's rescue center, which is supported by PETA's Global Compassion Fund. There, he dug into a bowl of nutritious puppy food and, perhaps for the first time, ate until he was full. Intensive veterinary care and a regimen of vitamins and other nutritional support—plus a much-needed bath—worked wonders for Mogli, and he grew visibly stronger and healthier with each passing day.

No longer having to worry about scavenging for his next meal or dodging traffic, Mogli was finally free to be a puppy. He made fast friends with two other pups at the rescue center, and the three of them spent their days playing, romping, and wrestling before flopping into an exhausted heap for a nap.

Soon, Mogli was ready to go to his permanent

home with a PETA Germany staff member. Today, he's healthy and strong. He no longer crawls but runs with abandon. Now, his "security blanket" is his loving guardian, and he's never far from her side. The tattered paper cup may still be out there somewhere, blowing around in the wind, but Mogli doesn't need it anymore. Nowadays, his cup runneth over.

"Kindness and compassion towards all living things is a mark of a civilized society. ... Only when we have become nonviolent towards all life will we have learned to live well ourselves."

—César Chávez

Chapter 9

A LIFESAVING DETOUR

From the window of the Jeep she was riding in, PETA President Ingrid Newkirk could see that something wasn't right. Nomads were moving a flock of sheep along a dusty dirt road—not an uncommon sight in rural India. But instead of trotting along as healthy sheep might, some of them were limping badly, struggling to keep up.

"We'd better stop and have a look," Ingrid said, and the driver nodded. They were on their way to a meeting with Animal Rahat. But the meeting would have to wait.

As they got closer to the sheep, one of the Animal Rahat veterinarians traveling with the group quickly determined that four of the animals were severely lame and couldn't bear any weight on their afflicted legs. Taking even a few steps was excruciatingly painful for them. The only reason they were still walking on the hard-packed earth likely was because the boys herding them kept poking them with sticks. One heavily pregnant sheep had a young lamb clinging to her side, and she looked as if she were ready to give birth at any time.

The team thought fast. They politely introduced themselves to the sheep's owner and informed him of the animals' dire condition. Pooling the money they had on hand, they offered to buy the four sheep and the lamb and take them to Animal Rahat's sanctuary. The man accepted, and soon the group was sharing their Jeep with a flock of five. It was money well spent!

The rescue came just in time: The very next day, at Animal Rahat's sanctuary, the pregnant sheep, Rekha, delivered twin lambs. She was in such poor health that despite the veterinarians' expert care, neither of her lambs survived. Rekha likely would have died, too, if she had been forced to give birth out on that hot, dirty road. But with intensive veterinary care, nourishing food, rest, and plenty of love, the grieving mother and her older lamb, Shiva, began to recover, both physically and emotionally.

A lifetime of neglect had taken its toll on one of the other sheep, leaving her in severe pain from a chronically dislocated hip joint. After a careful assessment, the veterinarians determined that the kindest thing they could do for her was to give her a peaceful end to her suffering.

In the meantime, flockmates Sunita and Bhanu began to heal, trust, and thrive. As their legs grew stronger, they were soon ready to venture out of their barn and graze in the fields. They loved soaking up the sunshine and spent many hours relaxing together. But their story doesn't end there.

48

At the time of the sheep's rescue, Animal Rahat had just acquired 28 acres of land in India's picturesque Nilgiri Hills and was building a new sanctuary there, with a spacious shelter and fencing to protect the animals. The team knew that the soft earth would be perfect for the recovering sheep's sensitive legs. So the little herd of sheep was transported there, and they quickly befriended the horses, ponies, and donkeys who also share their lush green home.

Three months later, Rekha passed away of natural causes. She spent the last days of her life being treated with kindness and respect and watching her lamb grow healthy and strong—all because someone had cared enough to stop and help.

Chapter 10

MIRABELLA AND THE MIRACLE KITTENS

❝ The kittens stay there until they *die*," the irate man snarled over the phone to a PETA Germany staffer.

The man's young nephew—who clearly had much more empathy than his older family member—had called PETA Germany's rescue team earlier, begging for help. Breathlessly, the boy explained that the kittens' mother had been hit by a car and had died and the boy's unhinged uncle had locked the kittens in an attic to starve to death.

The PETA Germany staff member was now trying in vain to change the man's mind, but he refused to free the four kittens so that his nephew could feed them. There was no choice but to send a team to the family's farm and hope it wasn't too late.

At first, the man simply would not relent and stuck to his cruel plan. But PETA Germany is nothing if not persistent. When the team's appeal for compassion didn't work, they switched gears, laying out the consequences that the man would face from authorities if he deliberately allowed the animals to starve to death. That did the trick.

The staffers picked up the kittens, who were clinging to life, and rushed them to PETA Germany's rescue center. At just 2 weeks old, they should have been nursing every few hours, but it had been far longer than that since they had eaten. PETA Germany's team did their best, bottle-feeding the malnourished and dehydrated kittens day and night, cuddling them, and keeping them warm and comfortable. But we all know that nothing can replace a mother's love.

That's where Mirabella came in.

PETA Germany had rescued Mirabella, a calico cat, from a hard life on the streets, where she had been scavenging for scraps of food. The team had already lined up a loving home for her, and she was staying at the rescue center while she recovered from her spay surgery. Knowing that she possessed a gentle and loving nature, the rescue team decided to put the kittens in her room overnight.

By the next morning, the kittens were no longer orphans: Mirabella had adopted them! All four kittens were contentedly snuggled up against her in their basket. She affectionately groomed them and enveloped them with love, as any good mother would.

With the blessing of Mirabella's future guardian, this new family stayed together at PETA Germany's rescue center for a few more weeks. Mirabella patiently taught her new charges how to eat solid food, use a litterbox, groom themselves, and do everything else that growing kittens need to learn. Under her doting care, the kittens thrived. When they were old enough, PETA Germany sterilized them and placed them in adoptive homes of their own.

One more good thing came of all this. Before they whisked the starving kittens to safety, the rescue team had managed to persuade the reluctant uncle to allow them to come back to spay and neuter two other cats and a dog who lived on the farm. PETA Germany does the same for many other animals living in rural and impoverished areas—preventing countless kittens and puppies from being born into a world where they aren't welcome.

And just as Mirabella taught her kittens, PETA Germany teaches young people to have compassion for all sentient beings, by holding animal-care workshops and making humane education a permanent part of school curricula. The group is working hard to ensure that the next generation is less like the cruel uncle and more like the caring nephew who refused to turn his back on four helpless kittens.

Chapter 11

LEADING
A WATER
BUFFALO TO
WATER

Male water buffaloes grow to be the size of a small car, weighing more than 2,600 pounds when they're fully grown. But a young water buffalo calf named Kalu was so small at the time of his rescue that he fit inside a basket on the back of a bicycle. And that's exactly how he arrived at Animal Rahat's sanctuary, taken there by a kind person who had saved him from going to a slaughterhouse.

Weak, anemic, and nothing but skin and bones, Kalu likely wouldn't have survived much longer if not for the expert care that he received from the staff of Animal Rahat.

In India, water buffaloes are often treated as living tractors—forced to plow fields or haul heavy carts in the hot sun day after day. Female water buffaloes are exploited for their milk, much as cows are in the U.S. They're chained for life in factory-like dairies, and their beloved calves are torn away from them soon after birth so that humans can consume the milk that rightfully belongs to them.

That's most likely what happened to Kalu. Worthless to dairy farmers, male calves are either turned out into the streets or slaughtered. Or maybe he was destined to plow someone's field but was cast off because his owner couldn't afford the veterinary care he needed. Maybe someone just couldn't see the value of a weak little calf. But Animal Rahat's staffers did. They got right to work nursing the sick baby back to health—not so that he could be put to work one day but so that he could grow up to live a happy and fulfilling life.

Round-the-clock bottle feedings quickly built up Kalu's strength. Soon, he was investigating, then nibbling, then enthusiastically *devouring* the fresh green grass fed to the cows, bullocks, horses, and camels at Animal Rahat's sanctuary.

Although he was the only water buffalo at the sanctuary at the time, Kalu's outgoing personality quickly won him friends of all species. He grew up frolicking with donkey foals who were close to his age, and as he got bigger, he mingled and play-fought with two patient adult bullocks named Parshya and Sonya. When caretakers took the camels for their daily walks, Kalu would call out and jump up and down to get their attention.

Kalu's fun-loving personality grew brighter each day, and he developed a bit of a mischievous streak. After his meals, he loves to pick up his empty food trough with his horns and toss it around like a toy. When his caretakers gave him a car tire to play with, he lifted it up on his forehead and threw it back at them!

He relished his new life, but one thing was missing. As their name implies, water buffaloes *love* water. And while the sanctuary had self-grooming stations, mineral-rich salt licks, and shady shelters for the residents, it didn't have a pond deep enough for Kalu to immerse himself. So he made do with wallowing in mud puddles, and sanctuary staffers showered him daily with fresh water. The cool, refreshing spray felt so wonderful on his skin that he would jump around with glee. But he still didn't have the one thing that he yearned for more than anything else: a pond.

Then one day, his life changed again. Animal Rahat had just finished building a new, larger sanctuary, and the torrential downpours that flood India during monsoon season created a natural pond there, just perfect for swimming! Kalu was transferred to the new sanctuary—although this time, on a truck instead of in a basket on a bike—and the entire staff gathered near the pond to see how he would react. He didn't need any prompting. He was almost immediately fully submerged, splashing, rolling around, shaking his head, and swimming joyfully, as he had always dreamed of doing. The staff clapped and cheered him on.

Kalu has settled in at the sanctuary, where he

now has other water buffalo pals, and shows his gratitude and affection for his caretakers by running up to them for his grooming sessions. And of course, he never misses a day of hanging out in "his" pond—although he's generous enough to share it with the other animals who also call the sanctuary home.

"[W]e share with other animals the same desire to live, to have a family, to love, and to die without violence."

—Jeffrey Moussaieff Masson

Chapter 12

FROM LAB TO LAP: THREE SISTERS' JOURNEY

S ome of the first things you might notice if you were to meet Peggy, Sarah, and Siri—three happy, playful rat sisters—are the large half-moons of flesh missing from their delicate ears. These scars are telltale reminders that the sisters endured a painful past at the Cleveland Clinic, a U.S. National Institutes of Health (NIH)–funded laboratory where rats and mice are subjected to invasive brain experiments.

The animals who end up there aren't treated like the unique individuals they are but rather like test tubes with whiskers. They aren't given names, only numbers. To identify them, experimenters do something terrible: They punch holes in their sensitive ears and attach cumbersome metal tags.

During a six-month undercover investigation inside Cleveland Clinic laboratories, PETA documented the horrible things that hundreds of millions of taxpayer dollars are funding.

A warning: This is gruesome but important to know. Experimenters mutilated mice by cutting open their heads, drilling into their skulls, and vacuuming out portions of their brains to expose the hippocampus. Then they covered the gaping wound with a piece of glass and glued it in place with a stainless steel "head cap" that was mounted onto the animals' skulls.

Why did they do this? Apparently, so that they could monitor "the brain condition." In other words, just to see what happens. But it's well known that the anatomy and physiology of the mouse brain and the anatomy and physiology of the human brain are very different and that such experiments don't teach us anything useful for human health. Rats and mice are the preferred victims not for any scientific reason but because they're cheap to breed and easy to exploit. And because of flagrant speciesism, these misunderstood and much-maligned little animals—when kept in laboratories—are specifically excluded from the Animal Welfare Act, the *only* federal law offering any sort of protection for animals in laboratories.

That's why, in one experiment at the Cleveland Clinic, lab workers were allowed to deny mice pain relief after they had been deliberately bred to suffer from pelvic organ prolapses—in which the uterus, bladder, or rectal tissue sags down and even protrudes out of the body. One mouse named Daisy had bloody, protruding rectal tissue that she dragged through her bedding for 10 weeks before she was finally gassed to death.

And that's not all. Experimenters injected mice with a chemical that left them struggling to walk and dragging their hind legs, then cut into their backs and separated their muscles from their vertebrae so that they could take images of their spinal cords.

Rats and mice are extremely social, communicating with each other using high-frequency sounds that humans can't hear without special instruments. They play, wrestle, and sleep all curled up together. However, at the Cleveland Clinic, not only do animals endure excruciating physical pain, their psychological needs are also completely ignored.

Rats can recognize expressions of pain on other rats' faces and react to them. Just like humans, if they don't have companionship, they can become lonely, anxious, and depressed. Yet some rats at the Cleveland Clinic are kept in solitary confinement, with nothing but a paper towel for "enrichment." Others are crammed into severely crowded cages, which leads to fights and causes newborns to be trampled and attacked by severely stressed adults.

But Peggy, Sarah, and Siri got away. PETA's investigator rescued them, allowing them to leave the Cleveland Clinic's cruelty far behind. Now, safe in a comfortable home with a loving guardian, their personalities are blossoming.

Despite being the smallest, Peggy is the adventurer. She never lets her tiny size stop her—she just *has* to climb higher and investigate new toys faster than her sisters do. She's the "baby sister" of the group and acts extra sassy. Siri is very playful and inquisitive. She loves being tickled and gently wrestling with her guardian's fingers. Sarah is the nurturer. While her sisters are out swinging on toys, she can often be found "redecorating" the nest with tissue and timothy hay. When she's given a treat, she always shares it with her sisters.

Instead of wasting away in a laboratory cage, these rats spend their days burrowing, building nests, snuggling in soft bedding, snacking on fresh fruits and veggies, climbing all over their guardian, and napping inside her hoodie.

PETA works hard to stop cruel experiments like those at the Cleveland Clinic so that one day *all* rats and mice can experience the bliss of being loved and the freedom of being themselves.

"[M]an and the other animals are all alike as to mental machinery, and there isn't any difference of any stupendous magnitude between them, except in quality, not in kind."

—Mark Twain

Chapter 13

THE ACCIDENTAL DONKEY

Lavender doesn't know what she's missing—and that's a good thing. She's a donkey foal who spends her days running, playing, and relaxing with her mother and other donkeys under swaying treetops in India's picturesque Nilgiri Hills. It's the kind of life every donkey longs for and deserves, and it's the only life she has ever known.

But Lavender was nearly born into an entirely different life. Her mother was one of the thousands of donkeys used as "beasts of burden" at India's sweltering brick kilns, where they're forced to haul massive loads of bricks until they quite literally drop from exhaustion. There is no peaceful retirement for them at the end of a hard life: Often, they're butchered for their skin and flesh or simply left by the roadside to die.

Donkeys are gregarious, inquisitive, affectionate, and social. Under natural conditions, they enjoy living in tight-knit herds. And although they may be small, they're also strong, courageous, and stoic, working without complaint even when suffering from chafing wounds or aching joints and parched from dehydration. These traits make them ripe for exploitation, and in India's brick kilns, they're beaten, goaded, and bullied into almost supernatural feats of strength and endurance. They receive little, if any, respite from the scorching heat as they trudge along under their extraordinarily heavy loads.

Lavender's mother had it even worse than most—not only was she being forced to carry loads of more than 200 pounds of bricks at a time without sufficient rest, food, or water to sustain her, she was also forced to do it while pregnant.

She had no way of knowing it, but her days of backbreaking toil were about to come to an end, thanks to Animal Rahat.

Animal Rahat veterinarians and other staff members regularly visit the country's brick kilns to provide the overworked donkeys with the basic medical care that they are denied, such as vaccinations, wound treatment, and much-needed hoof trimming. They counsel donkey owners about proper care and persuade them to construct corrals and sheds to shelter the animals and free them from being hobbled or tightly tethered by the legs.

Perhaps most important of all, Animal Rahat works to eliminate the need to offer this vital service in the first place, by encouraging brick kiln operators to use tractors and other motorized vehicles to haul heavy loads instead of long-suffering donkeys, emphasizing the cost- and time-saving benefits of mechanization as well as the incalculable humanitarian gains.

It was thanks to Animal Rahat's outreach that five brick kilns decided to replace donkeys with tractors, enabling the organization to retire Lavender's mother and 74 other donkeys from the daily exhausting labor.

During a post-rescue examination, an Animal Rahat veterinarian discovered that Lavender's mother was pregnant. Just days later, she gave birth to Lavender, a spunky, precocious ball of gray fuzz who captured everyone's hearts with her antics.

By rescuing her mother just in the nick of time, Animal Rahat ensured that Lavender will never experience the misery of forced labor in a brick kiln. Instead, she can relish life at Animal Rahat's partner sanctuary, playfully nibbling on her mother's ears, rolling on her back and kicking up her heels to create big plumes of dust, and frolicking in lush fields with other rescued donkeys. In short, she is enjoying the safety, comfort, and loving care that she was very nearly deprived of, and she will never be forced to haul anything, not even a pebble.

Chapter 14

THE SULTAN OF PETRA

Sultans traditionally live in palaces, but the Sultan of this story spent his days and nights outdoors, curled up on the carved stone steps of an amphitheater in the ancient city of Petra, Jordan, the only "home" the stray puppy ever knew.

It was there that a PETA U.K. staffer, Theodora Iona—who was visiting Petra to help set up PETA's free veterinary clinic for the donkeys, horses, and camels forced to haul vacationers around the tourist attraction—spotted Sultan surrounded by a group of children.

Theodora quickly realized that the children weren't playing with the puppy. Instead, they were taunting and viciously kicking him. Gentle soul that he is, Sultan simply endured the abuse without so much as a growl or a nip to defend himself. As Theodora rushed to intervene, the children scattered. That's when she noticed that Sultan couldn't have run away from his attackers even if he had tried: One leg was so badly injured that he couldn't put any weight on it.

Fearing that Sultan's leg was broken, Theodora

bundled him into her car and whisked him off to the closest veterinarian available at the time. Miraculously, his leg was not broken, but it was badly bruised and swollen. The vet prescribed anti-inflammatory medication and recommended that the injured leg be massaged daily.

Theodora took him back to her rental apartment, which was quickly turning into a makeshift animal shelter as she encountered animals in need of help. First, there was a stray kitten named Aicha. Then came puppies Mia and Rosie, the latter of whom was seriously ill with parvovirus (a deadly infectious disease that spreads quickly in impoverished areas where dogs aren't commonly vaccinated). Parvo is usually a death sentence, and several puppies Theodora rescued had succumbed to it. Rosie, however, was a different story: Despite her delicate stature, she possessed a constitution of steel, and with a few weeks of TLC, she eventually made a full recovery.

Nobody fought like cats and dogs—in fact, Sultan and Aicha became fast friends. They loved to play and snuggle with each other, even during the long car rides to and from the closest humane society four hours away, where Theodora took them to get sterilized, vaccinated, and microchipped.

Just as his name suggests, Sultan is a natural leader, and when PETA opened its vital, free veterinary clinic in Petra, he became an essential member of the team, acting as a "therapy dog" for nervous equine patients. Clinic workers quickly noticed that Sultan had a special bond with donkeys, communicating with them in ways humans couldn't comprehend and somehow keeping them calm while they underwent examinations and treatment.

In fact, while Sultan is a loving and protective big brother to Mia and Rosie, his very best friend at the clinic is undoubtedly Buzz, a donkey who lives there permanently after enduring extreme abuse at the hands of his previous owner. Buzz and Sultan can often be found contentedly sitting in the sand in the clinic's rehabilitation area, leaning on each other. Whenever Sultan seeks out a shady spot to escape the midday sun, Buzz follows along to nuzzle and groom him while he naps.

Sultan relishes every moment of his life at PETA's clinic, which—in addition to treating donkeys, horses, and camels for lameness, saddle sores, skin infections, and other injuries—helps dogs like him with conditions such as mange, snakebites, maggot-infested wounds, and malnutrition. And when the clinic conducts vital community outreach, counseling local residents—including children—on the importance of respecting and properly caring for animals, Sultan is right there, listening. The staff have even recruited some children to help groom and feed the animals at the clinic, including a teenage volunteer who proudly tells everyone that the clinic has saved dozens of animals' lives. The Sultan of Petra approves.

Chapter 15

How Woody Got out of the Woods

Driving down long stretches of rural Australian highway can get monotonous pretty quickly. Country roads Down Under feature swaths of forest interspersed with long patches of towering grass and little else. But one day, something caught the eye of a PETA Australia supporter as she was driving: a sheep, lying all alone, at the edge of a pasture. She could swear that the last time she drove down this stretch of highway—five days earlier—she had seen the same sheep lying in the same spot.

Sheep are highly social animals who like to stay with their flocks—they feel afraid and their hearts beat faster if they're separated from their family and others they know. Something didn't seem right about this solitary sheep, so the driver let compassion take the wheel and pulled over to investigate.

She was greeted by a tragic sight: The ewe was dead. She had apparently been struggling to stand up for so long that her attempts to right herself had left an indentation in the ground around her—a "snow angel" in the grass, wrought out of despair. Who knows how long this poor ewe had suffered before she died, unnoticed and unmourned. But then a movement caught the woman's eye: Next to the dead sheep lay her baby, still desperately trying to suckle from his mother's lifeless body.

The little lamb had no chance of surviving without his mother, so the kind woman gently scooped him up, placed him in the backseat of her car, and sped off to a veterinarian.

An examination revealed that at only a few weeks old, the lamb already had several health problems from his difficult start in life. His mother had no doubt tried her best to feed him, but her depleted body couldn't produce enough of the milk that he needed to thrive. Now he had an excess buildup of acid in his empty stomach, and it had created a painful ulcer. He was going to need extensive veterinary care and medication if he had any hope of recovering. But thankfully, the woman who rescued him was happy to provide both.

She took him home to begin his recovery. At first, he was desperate to drink as much as possible, eagerly draining bottle after bottle. And who could blame him, after being hungry for so long? And he started to gain strength, but progress came slowly. When friends and family asked for updates, they were told, "We're not out of the woods yet." And that's how this determined lamb came to be called "Woody."

As Woody's rescuer nursed him back to health, she thought about the millions upon millions of sheep and lambs who aren't as fortunate and experience nothing but suffering at human hands. In Australia's wool industry, thousands of sheep—far too many for farmers to care for properly—are raised on massive ranches. They suffer from all kinds of ailments and injuries that go untreated, and shearers (who are often cruel, impatient, angry, and sometimes even high on amphetamines) callously toss them around, kick and stomp on them, slam their heads into the ground, and cut their delicate skin during rough, careless shearing.

When sheep become older and less "productive," they are no longer useful to farmers, so they're sent on a frightening journey to slaughter. Many are packed onto open-deck, multitier ships and sent thousands of miles across the ocean in all weather conditions, mired in their own waste and often unable to reach food or water because of the severe crowding. Many don't survive the journey, but those who do will end up with their throats cut soon after they reach their destination.

Thanks to a kind person's intervention, though, Woody will never have to endure such horrors. His rescuer decided to make him a permanent member of her family, and today, he's healthy, happy, and all healed up. With every passing day, he reveals more of his huge personality and sense of fun.

Just like a companion dog or cat, Woody has

unique quirks and daily rituals, like bleating a demand for breakfast at exactly the same time every morning. He expresses his delight by jumping with all four feet off the ground and spinning 360 degrees in the air. He is also an avid soccer player, although he has not yet learned how to kick the ball without tipping over!

Like Woody, all animals have so much to live for, and they deserve to experience joy and pleasure. Sometimes they just need a little help to get out of the woods.

"To my mind the life of a lamb is no less precious than that of a human being. ... I hold that, the more helpless a creature, the more entitled it is to protection by man from the cruelty of man."

—Mahatma Gandhi

"*[E]verything* we do matters. If we all support each other in our dream of justice and kindness— and we reflect that dream in our daily acts—we can each be our own Rosa Parks."

—Gloria Steinem

Chapter 16

YOU CAN MAKE A DIFFERENCE!

As the stories in this book show, one person truly can make a difference! So many lives have been saved, improved, and changed forever—all because one person cared enough to step in, speak up, and get involved. Will you be that "one person" for animals in need?

All around the world, animals are forced to haul heavy loads, imprisoned far from their families and homes, subjected to the agony of having their skin torn off for fashion, caged, poisoned, experimented on in laboratories, killed for a nugget or a burger, and deprived of everything that makes their lives worth living.

Animals need people to speak up and share the facts: that animals exist for their own purposes, not for human convenience. When people begin to understand that all animals are sentient individuals with unique personalities and with families and feelings and that they value their lives as much as we value ours, it becomes impossible to justify exploiting them.

There are endless ways, large and small, to help people understand *who* animals are and how to live compassionately every day. If you're ready to help animals, here are a few ideas to get you started, but don't stop with these. Every kind act contributes to making a world of difference for animals.

Help End Animal Exploitation for Entertainment Around the Globe

- Give animals a holiday—never ride donkeys, camels, or horses at tourist attractions. The same goes for elephants, who are torn away from their mothers as babies, chained, and beaten to make them submissive.

- Reject "swim with dolphins" programs. Captive dolphins live in misery long after travelers return home with their photos. To dolphins and other marine mammals, even the largest swimming pool is a prison, and interactions with humans wreak havoc on their physical and psychological well-being.

- Urge everyone you know to reject bullfights and the Running of the Bulls while vacationing in countries where such atrocities still take place. Sign PETA's petition to end these cruel spectacles at **PETA.org/Bullfighting**.

- Never pose for photos with wild animals like monkeys or parrots or lion, tiger, or bear cubs. Baby animals used for photo ops are torn away from their mothers when they're just a few days old. When they grow up and become too difficult to handle, many are relegated to cramped cages or even sold to hunting ranches to be shot and killed.

- Beware of pseudo-sanctuaries, or roadside zoos that pose as "sanctuaries" or "rescues" and claim to support species conservation in order to attract customers. Only visit reputable sanctuaries—go to PETA.org for ways to tell the difference. Observe animals in their natural habitat by going birdwatching or hiking, and check out the many stunning nature documentaries that give you an up-close look at all kinds of animals.

- If you're planning to travel with your animal companions, never risk loss, injury, or death by flying them in the cargo hold of a plane, which can be terrifying to them and cause injuries and even death if luggage shifts or temperature controls or air pressure systems malfunction. See PETA.org for tips to make sure that your trip is safe for *everyone*.

- If you live in a city where horse-drawn carriage rides are still legal, campaign to get them banned. Contact PETA for step-by-step instructions. And refuse to ride in horse-drawn carriages if you visit Charleston, South Carolina; Kolkata, India; Berlin; Vienna; or anywhere else they're offered.

- Urge everyone you know—and even those you don't (via social media)—to avoid SeaWorld and other *abuse*ment parks, which imprison marine mammals in barren concrete tanks, leading to depression, aggression, and self-destructive behavior caused by the stress of captivity.

- Never attend circuses that force animals to perform. Support awe-inspiring animal-free circuses, such as Cirque du Soleil and Cirque Éloize, which use only willing human performers who can quit if they so desire.

- Teach children that it's wrong to tear animals away from their families and homes and put them on display for our amusement, such as by keeping fish in aquariums or birds in cages. For free, fun, and age-appropriate educational materials about animal rights issues, visit **PETA.org/Teachkind**.

Be an Animal's Best Friend

- Make an emergency plan for your animal companions *before* a disaster strikes. Keep an evacuation kit packed with all the essentials: their veterinary records, medications, food, water bowl, carrier, leash, harness, and litterbox (for cats) as well as a list of animal-friendly hotels.

- Keep a list of animal shelters, rescue groups, and veterinarians in your phone in case you spot a stray or an injured animal. Be sure to keep a rescue kit in your car—learn how to assemble one at PETA.org.

- Volunteer to walk dogs or play with cats at your local animal shelter. Help busy staff by cleaning cages or doing other chores. You can also help by donating blankets, towels, toys, cat litter, food, and other supplies.

- Post information about low-cost spay/neuter services on social media, and explain why animals need to be sterilized to stop overpopulation and homelessness.

- Take immediate action if you see an animal left alone in a hot vehicle—it's an emergency! Note the car's color, model, make, and license plate number. Have the owner paged in nearby buildings, and/or call local humane authorities or police. Stay until help arrives. If the animal's life is in immediate danger, carefully get him or her out of the vehicle and to a veterinarian as soon as possible. See PETA.org for more tips.

- Offer to walk neighbors' dogs who are left alone during the day. They would surely enjoy some company and exercise—not to mention a bathroom break!

- If your local newspaper runs "free to a good home" advertisements, warn the editors that cruel people looking for free animals to abuse and those who sell animals to laboratories for experiments are known to obtain them this way. Ask newspapers to stop running these ads, and call people who place them to warn them of the danger.

Save Animals' Skin

- Show people that wool isn't "just a haircut" by sharing the disturbing footage from PETA's wool investigations (available at PETA.org) on social media. Encourage others to choose humane fabrics, such as cotton, polyester, nylon, or rayon, rather than wool.

- Shop for cruelty-free fashions, and urge stores not to sell bags, belts, coats, shoes, or anything else made out of the skin of snakes, lizards, alligators, cows, or any other animals.

- Don't buy bedding, pillows, or clothing filled

with down feathers—which are violently torn out of the skin of ducks and geese. Visit PETA.org to see footage from goose farms and learn about cruelty-free, eco-friendly fill.

• Clear your closet and your conscience of fur: If you have one, donate your fur coat and any other fur items to PETA! We'll put them to good use by giving them to a wildlife rehabilitator for bedding or to a homeless person for warmth or by using them in educational events.

Be a Caring Consumer

• If you're a U.S. resident, visit **PETA.org/NIHWaste** to demand that the National Institutes of Health stop wasting your tax dollars on cruel experimentation, such as cranial window experiments on mice and rats at the Cleveland Clinic.

• Choose cosmetics, toiletries, and household products that haven't been tested on animals, and tell companies that conduct experiments on animals that you won't buy their products until they stop. You can find a list of companies that do and that don't test on animals at PETA.org.

• Only support health charities that spend their time and money on relevant programs that can really help save lives—not ones that fund or conduct inhumane and wasteful animal experiments.

Viva Vegan!

- Going vegan is the best thing you can do to help the greatest number of animals. Each vegan saves nearly 200 animals every year.

- Take nonperishable vegan food items like oatmeal, rice, beans, and aseptic boxes of vegan milk to your local food bank to help animals as well as families in need.

- Donate to a vegan hunger-relief organization, such as Food for Life Global or A Well-Fed World, to help hungry humans while promoting vegan living and sparing the lives of cows, pigs, chickens, turkeys, fish, and other animals.

- Leave a stack of vegan starter kits at doctors' offices, grocery stores, airports, and anywhere else you go. PETA can send you a supply.

- Take vegan dishes to potlucks, office parties, bake sales, and other functions. Share animal-friendly recipes—there are hundreds at PETA.org—and let everyone know where to find tasty vegan meals and goodies.

- Ask local schools to offer more vegan options in their cafeterias.

Never Be Silent

- Never assume that "someone else will help." If you see a suffering animal, you are probably that animal's only hope, so take action. Call the police, animal control, or PETA for help, if needed.

- Let companies and policymakers know how you feel about their actions—both good and bad—that involve animals. Ask them to introduce vegan products and compassionate policies or to support animal-friendly legislation.

- Download PETA's app and take part in our action alerts. Encourage your friends and family to join you.

- Urge people to liberate their language and stop using violent and offensive sayings, such as "kill two birds with one stone" or "bring home the bacon." When writing or speaking, never label animals in ways that make it easier to rationalize or normalize cruelty (such as referring to them as "laboratory animals," "zoo animals," "circus animals," or "food animals").

- Wear T-shirts and buttons with animal rights messages, or put an animal rights bumper sticker or personalized license plate on your car. Little things can have a big impact.

- Get active without leaving your armchair: Write letters to the editors of newspapers, call radio talk shows to tell the host and the audience about relevant animal rights issues, and post comments on social media if a character in a TV program or movie abuses or ridicules animals.

- Alert PETA or the appropriate authorities if you witness cruelty or the neglect of an animal in a pet store, circus, roadside zoo, factory farm, laboratory, or anywhere else.

- Add an animal rights quote (see page 45 for an example) to your e-mail auto-signature or other correspondence.

Live in Harmony With Wildlife

- Carry reusable tote bags when shopping to reduce waste and help save wildlife habitat and marine animals, who can mistake plastic bags for food and eat them, often leading to death.

- If you see turtles trying to cross the road, carry

them safely across in the direction that they were headed—if you take them back to the side where they started out, they will venture back out into the road again to proceed to their original destination.

- Create a mini-sanctuary for birds, butterflies, and other animals by keeping part of your yard natural, planting native shrubs, trees, and wildflowers that benefit animals and insects, and adding nesting boxes, seasonal feeders, and a fresh water source.

- If your apartment or office building is using glue traps, tell the building manager that these traps are cruel and dangerous and urge him or her to use humane alternatives.

Share the Wealth

- If you're in a position to do so, please contribute to PETA's Global Compassion Fund, which supports the life-changing work of diverse animal protection groups around the world. Go to **PETA.org/GCF** for more details.

- Want to help PETA's investigators expose—and stop—cruelty to animals, as well as assisting PETA in providing animals with emergency veterinary treatment, transport, and shelter? You can, by supporting our Investigations & Rescue Fund. Visit **PETA.org/IRF** to learn more.

- Visit **AnimalRahat.com** to find out how you can sponsor a rescued animal in India.

- Sponsor a spay or neuter surgery at PETA's mobile SNIP (Spay or Neuter Immediately, Please!) clinic, or provide a dog who is forced to live outside in the bitter cold without shelter with a custom-built, straw-filled doghouse from PETA. See PETA.org to make one—or both—of these lifesaving gifts!

"The worst sin towards our fellow creatures is not to hate them, but to be indifferent to them: that's the essence of inhumanity."

—George Bernard Shaw

Epilogue

As you were reading about the animal rescues described in this book, you may have thought to yourself, *How does PETA do it? How can one organization save so many animals all over the world?* The answer is—we can't. That is, we can't do it alone. We rely on the help of kind people who are determined to stop cruelty wherever it occurs, from sheep farms in Chile to slaughterhouses in China.

That's why PETA established the Global Compassion Fund, which works all over the world to improve and save animals' lives where help is needed the most, including in the following places:

- In the Philippines, in a Manila cemetery, where deeply impoverished families live with their animals among the tombs, PETA Asia provides dogs and cats in need with emergency veterinary care, vaccinations, and other vital services.
- In Romania, PETA Germany sterilizes homeless dogs and cats, reducing the number fending for themselves on the streets.
- In Mexico, PETA has rescued dogs from the streets and sterilized hundreds of them.
- In India, PETA India has rescued bullocks, donkeys, ponies, and many species of wildlife from deep wells, forced labor, and even slaughter.

Each act is wonderful and heartwarming, and each is directly supported by PETA's Global Compassion Fund.

I hope reading this book has inspired you to support the fund (**PETA.org/GCF**) and to help power *all* our grassroots programs that are making a world of difference for animals.

—Ingrid

"Our task must be to free ourselves ... by widening our circle of compassion to embrace all living creatures and the whole of nature in its beauty."

—Albert Einstein